EXECUTIVE OFFICE OF THE PRESIDENT
NATIONAL ECONOMIC COUNCIL
OFFICE OF SCIENCE AND TECHNOLOGY POLICY

A STRATEGY FOR AMERICAN INNOVATION:
DRIVING TOWARDS SUSTAINABLE GROWTH AND QUALITY JOBS

> *History should be our guide. The United States led the world's economies in the 20th century because we led the world in innovation. Today, the competition is keener; the challenge is tougher; and that is why innovation is more important than ever. It is the key to good, new jobs for the 21st century. That's how we will ensure a high quality of life for this generation and future generations. With these investments, we're planting the seeds of progress for our country, and good-paying, private-sector jobs for the American people."*
>
> -President Barack Obama, August 5, 2009

SEPTEMBER 2009

EXECUTIVE SUMMARY

Since taking office, President Obama has taken historic steps to lay the foundation for the innovation economy of the future. The Obama Innovation Strategy builds on well over $100 billion of Recovery Act funds that support innovation, additional support for education, infrastructure and others in the Recovery Act and the President's Budget, and novel regulatory and executive order initiatives. It seeks to harness the inherent ingenuity of the American people and a dynamic private sector to ensure that the next expansion is more solid, broad-based, and beneficial than previous ones. It focuses on critical areas where sensible, balanced government policies can lay the foundation for innovation that leads to quality jobs and shared prosperity. It has three parts:

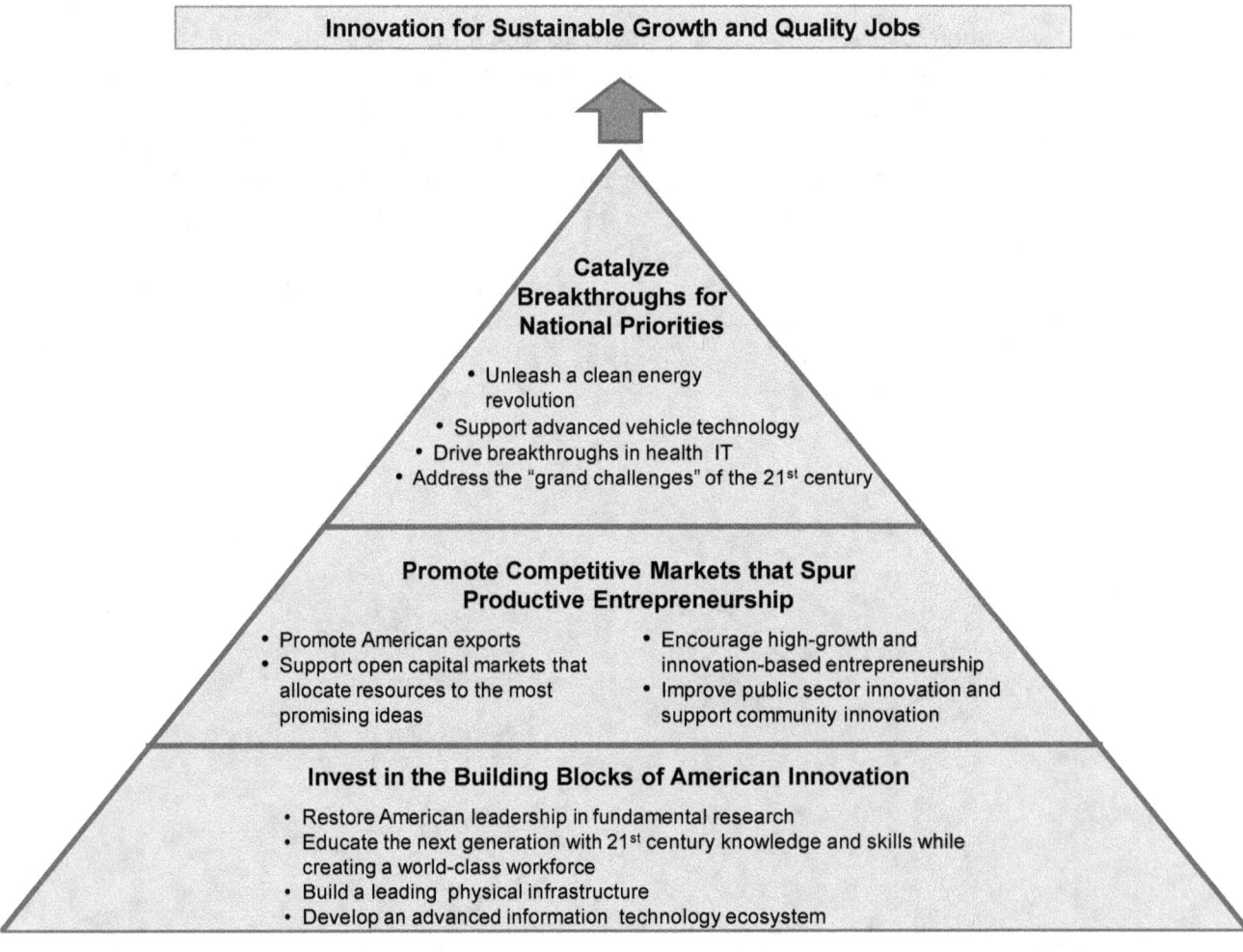

1. **Invest in the Building Blocks of American Innovation.** We must first ensure that our economy is given all the necessary tools for successful innovation, from investments in research and development to the human, physical, and technological capital needed to perform that research and transfer those innovations.

   - **Restore American leadership in fundamental research.** President Obama implemented the largest increase in basic R&D in history, which will lay the foundation for new discoveries and new technologies that will improve our lives and create the industries of the future.

- **Educate the next generation with 21st century knowledge and skills while creating a world-class workforce.** President Obama has proposed initiatives to dramatically improve teaching and learning in K-12 education, expand access to higher education and training, and promote student achievement and careers in STEM (Science, Technology, Engineering, and Mathematics) fields.
- **Build a leading physical infrastructure.** Through the Recovery Act, the President has committed to a historic investment in our nation's roads, bridges, transit, and air transportation networks to connect our people and our businesses.
- **Develop an advanced information technology ecosystem.** For America to lead the world in the technologies of the future, President Obama believes that all Americans must have affordable 21st century access to the Internet.

2. **Promote Competitive Markets that Spur Productive Entrepreneurship.** It is imperative to create a national environment ripe for entrepreneurship and risk taking that allows U.S. companies to be internationally competitive in a global exchange of ideas and innovation. Through competitive markets, innovations diffuse and scale appropriately across industries and globally.

- **Promote American exports.** Exports will play an increasingly critical role in the future of the American economy, and the President's plans will ensure fair and open markets for American producers.
- **Support open capital markets that allocate resources to the most promising ideas.** Open capital markets are one of the greatest strengths of the American economy, and the President is committed to making sure these markets work.
- **Encourage high-growth and innovation-based entrepreneurship.** The Obama Administration believes it is essential that entrepreneurs continue to create new and vibrant businesses that lead to new jobs and economic growth.
- **Improve public sector innovation and support community innovation.** Innovation must occur within all levels of society, including the government itself. The Obama Administration supports the broad adoption of community innovations that work and is committed to making government perform better and more efficiently, including by working more openly.

3. **Catalyze Breakthroughs for National Priorities.** There are certain sectors of exceptional national importance where the market is unlikely to produce the desirable outcomes on its own. These include developing alternative energy sources, reducing costs and improving lives with health IT, and manufacturing advanced vehicles. In these industries where markets may fail on their own, government can be part of the solution.

- **Unleash a clean energy revolution.** Historic investments in smart grid, energy efficiency, and renewable technologies like wind, solar, and biofuels will help unleash a wave of ingenuity and progress that creates jobs, grows our economy, and ends our dependence on oil.
- **Support advanced vehicle technologies.** Record battery grants announced last month are part of a concerted effort to place the U.S. on the cutting edge of advanced vehicle technology, from electric cars to biofuels to advanced combustion.

- **Drive innovations in health care technology.** The President's health IT initiative is designed to drive technological innovation that will help prevent medical errors, improve health care quality, reduce costs, and cement U.S. leadership of this emerging industry.
- **Harness science and technology to address the "grand challenges" of the 21st century.** The President's commitment to science and technology will allow the United States to set and meet ambitious goals, such as educational software that is as effective as a personal tutor and smart anti-cancer therapeutics that deliver drugs only to tumor cells.

I –PROBLEMS WITH THE BUBBLE-DRIVEN GROWTH OF THE PAST

A strong economy, but too reliant on precarious, bubble-driven growth, is unsustainable

Despite American economy's historic strength, our economic growth has rested for too long on an unstable foundation. Explosive growth in one sector of the economy has provided a short-term boost while masking long-term weaknesses. In the 1990s, the technology sector climbed to new heights. The tech-heavy NASDAQ composite index rose over 650 percent between 1995 and 2000, but then lost two-thirds of its value in a single year, triggering a painful recession.

After the tech bubble burst, a new one emerged in the housing and financial sectors. During the course of the decade, the formula for buying a house changed: instead of saving to buy their dream house, many Americans found they could take out loans that by traditional standards their incomes could not support. The financial sector willingly propped up real estate prices, funneling money into real estate and finding innovative ways to spread the credit risk throughout the economy. From 2000 through 2006, house prices doubled while the financial sector grew to account for fully 40 percent of all corporate profits.

This too proved to be unsustainable. House prices lost a quarter of their value in two and a half years. The housing decline and accompanying stock market collapse wiped out over $13 trillion in wealth in 18 months. The bursting of the bubble based on inflated home prices, maxed-out credit cards, over-leveraged banks, and overvalued assets wreaked havoc on the real economy, triggering what is expected to be the longest and deepest recession since World War II and driving the unemployment rate to its highest level in a quarter century.

This type of growth isn't just problematic when the bubble bursts, it is not entirely healthy even while it lasts. Between 2000 and 2007 the typical working-age household saw their income decline by nearly $2,000. As middle-class incomes sank, the incomes of the top one percent skyrocketed. This phenomenon has a number of causes, but among them were the rising asset prices and the proliferation of financial sector profits.

A short-term focus has neglected essential fundamental investments

A short-term view of the economy masks underinvestments in essential drivers of sustainable, broadly-shared growth. It promotes temporary fixes over lasting solutions. This is patently clear when looking at how education, infrastructure, healthcare, energy, and research – all pillars of lasting prosperity – were ignored during the last bubble.

Too many children are not getting the world class education they deserve and need to thrive in this new innovative economy.

- Despite research documenting that quality matters greatly in early childhood education settings and that investments in high-quality early learning have the highest potential rates of return, the Federal government lacks the level of investment needed to transform the quality of, and enhance access to, early education for our youngest children. Studies show a school readiness gap as early as kindergarten –and as wide as 60 points –between children from the highest socio-economic background and their less affluent peers.

- We have neglected to provide our children with the rigorous curriculum and instruction needed to prepare them for college and career. By the end of high school, African American and Latino students have math and reading skills equivalent to those of 8th grade white students. Across the nation, the students with the greatest need for a qualified and effective teacher are also exactly those students most likely to be taught by teachers who lack sufficient background in the subject they teach.
- The problems persist when students look toward continuing their education past high school. The average tuition and fees at public, four-year institutions rose 26 percent between the 2000-2001 school year and the 2008-2009 school year. As a result, while 94 percent of high school students in the top quintile of socioeconomic status continue on to post-secondary education, barely half of those in the bottom quintile do so.
- Given rising costs of four-year institutions, many Americans are turning to community colleges for quality higher education. Yet the Federal government has historically under-invested in community colleges, giving them one-third the level of support per full-time equivalent student that it gives to public four-year colleges.

Our physical and technological infrastructure has been neglected, threatening the ability of American businesses to compete with the rest of the world.

- The American Society of Civil Engineers grades our country's physical infrastructure as a "D." In 2007, drivers on our clogged highways and streets experienced over 4.2 billion hours of delay and wasted 2.8 billion gallons of fuel.
- The United States once led the world in broadband deployment, but now that leadership is in question. Wireless networks in many countries abroad are faster and more advanced than our own.
- Our electrical grid is still constructed around the same model employed immediately after World War II. Power interruptions and outages cost American individuals and businesses at least $80 billion each year.

Health care costs have been allowed to spiral out of control, squeezing individuals and businesses at a time when they are feeling pressure on all sides.

- Since 2000, health insurance premiums have increased about 60 percent, 20 times faster than the average worker's wage.
- At the same time, the number of uninsured Americans has jumped by 7 million to 46 million.
- Overall, healthcare is consuming an increasing amount of our Nation's resources. In 1970, healthcare expenditures were 7 percent of GDP; now they are 16 percent of GDP; at this rate they will hit 20 percent of GDP by 2017.

Our economy has remained dependent on fossil fuels, exposing consumers and businesses to harmful price shocks, threatening our economic and national security, and resulting in a missed opportunity to lead the clean energy economy of the future.

- Between 1999 and 2004, the production tax credit for renewable energy was allowed to expire on three separate occasions. In each subsequent year (2000, 2003, and 2004) new wind capacity additions in the U.S. fell by more than 75 percent from the year before.
- Instead of focusing on finding ever more fossil fuels, other countries made aggressive investments in renewable energy, creating jobs and growing domestic energy sources.

Furthermore, we have compounded the problem by ignoring essential investments in high-technology research that will drive future growth.

- Over the last four decades, Federal funding for the physical, mathematical, and engineering sciences has declined by half as a percent of GDP (from 0.25 percent to 0.13 percent) while other countries have substantially increased their research budgets.

Despite this underinvestment in key drivers of growth, the American economy remains the most dynamic, innovative, and resilient in the world. We still have world-class research universities, flexible labor markets, deep capital markets, and an energetic entrepreneurial culture. Americans are twice as likely as adults in Europe and Japan to start a business with the intention of growing it rapidly. We must redouble our efforts to give our world-leading innovators every chance to succeed. We cannot rest on our laurels while other countries catch up.

II –A VISION FOR INNOVATION, GROWTH, AND JOBS

Innovation is Necessary to Fuel Our Recovery

Amidst the worst recession since the great depression, the Administration's initial economic objective has been to rescue our economy. We have taken – and will continue to take – bold and aggressive steps to stabilize the financial system, jumpstart job growth, and get credit flowing again.

But as the economy begins to stabilize, we must move on from rescue to recovery. Reflecting on the lessons of the past, we must rebuild a new foundation for durable, sustainable economic growth.

Innovation and investment must be a pillar of this new foundation. The basis of competition and the nature of the economy have changed, and we must change with them. Twenty years ago, the United States was losing domestic manufacturing firms and was competing with other countries to sell its goods. Now, manufacturing and services have merged, knowledge is a key factor of production, and services we thought could only be provided in particular countries are available anywhere. We need new ideas to provide Americans with new jobs, new services that take advantage of our globally interconnected world, and new skills that improve our manufacturing capabilities (See Box 1). Other countries understand that innovation is fundamental to their economic well-being and are finding new ways to advance their innovation agendas. We can be even more ambitious, even more successful, and even more focused on building the essential sidewalks of innovation.

Box 1. The Importance of a National Innovation Strategy

Fundamentally, innovation is the development of new products, services, and processes. In our increasingly interconnected and globally competitive world economy, unleashing innovation is an essential component of a comprehensive economic strategy. As global competition erodes the return to traditional practices, the key to developing more jobs and more prosperity will be to create and deploy new products and processes. Put another way, the greatest job and value creators of the future will be activities, jobs, and even industries that don't exist yet today. The countries that catalyze their development will reap the greatest rewards.

Innovation is essential for creating new jobs in both high-tech and traditional sectors. In recent years, innovation has led to new jobs in high-tech and advanced manufacturing sectors as diverse as aerospace, nanotechnology, life sciences, and alternative energy. At the same time, innovations ripple through the economy, creating jobs for workers installing broadband networks, manufacturing biopharmaceuticals, and building advanced infrastructure.

A more innovative economy is a more productive and faster growing economy, with higher returns to workers and increases in living standards. America's average standard of living will double every 23 years if innovation catalyzes annual productivity growth of three percent, but it will take 70 years if productivity growth is only one percent. Currently, the U.S. enjoys a significant productivity advantage: one study calculates that the average productivity advantage of the United States over all other OECD countries as a group accounted for a full three quarters of the per capita income advantage the U.S. enjoys. Continued innovation in products, business practices, and technology is essential for extending our productivity gains.

Innovation is also crucial for maintaining the dynamism and resilience of our economy. Future challenges are impossible to predict, but what is certain is that an economy better able to switch gears, innovate solutions, and re-deploy old activities, jobs, and industries will be least susceptible to adversity.

Finally, innovation is itself the key to meeting some of the greatest challenges facing our nation and the world. It will be pivotal to ending our dependence on fossil fuels, helping Americans live longer, healthier lives, and protecting our freedom and our troops both at home and abroad.

Innovation is the key to global competitiveness, new and better jobs, a resilient economy, and the attainment of essential national goals. A strategy is clearly needed to direct our government's funding and regulatory decisions in order to capture the innovation opportunity.

Our Vision for American Innovation

Our vision of America's future is one where prosperity is built by skilled, productive workers and sound investments that will spread opportunity at home and allow this nation to lead the world in the technologies, innovation and discoveries that will shape the 21st century.

Innovation will create new jobs and catalyze broadly shared economic growth. The lives of every American will improve as innovations diffuse and scale throughout the economy, leading to breakthroughs in health, education, energy, transportation, information, and much more. We can set and meet grand challenges such as developing solar cells as cheap as paint, building anti-cancer drugs that spare healthy cells, and fitting the contents of the library of congress on a device the size of a sugar cube.

Sustained innovation will drive a dynamic evolution in the nation's workforce towards better paying jobs. American workers will continue to lead across a broad range of industries and sectors old and new, and will prosper accordingly. Workers making innovation-induced shifts to new jobs within and across industries will receive the transition and training support necessary to ensure no one is left behind.

The American economy is and will remain highly diversified. To a large extent these jobs of the future will be spread across major industries in a similar distribution to today's economy. As the Council of Economic Advisors described in a July report, one forecast that uses the most recent data available to project employment growth finds that the distribution of jobs across industries in the economy of 2020 will strongly resemble the distribution of 2008. Health and education services will see the most significant growth, while there will be proportionally fewer jobs in business and financial services as well as retail trade, in part because the growth in consumer spending is expected to slow. But by and large the picture is similar to today.

Box 2. The Transformation of the Semi-Conductor Industry

In the 1980s, the U.S. semiconductor industry lost its market share to Japanese competitors. But then it innovated its way back, replacing the old jobs in the dynamic-random-access-memory (DRAM) business with jobs producing microprocessors, digital signal processors, microcontrollers, and automotive semiconductors. Companies like Intel, Texas Instruments, and Motorola invested and succeeded, creating better jobs for hundreds of thousands of Americans. Throughout this shift to higher-value-added jobs, the total number of U.S. jobs in the industry held constant.

Of course, such forecasts are necessarily imperfect. They cannot capture the growth in industries that may not yet exist. For example, in the late 1980s there were no models that predicted the rapid growth of Internet-based information and computing services that now employ several million workers. Innovation in this sector –initially catalyzed and continuously supported by government investment –has made key contributions to our economy. Some experts estimate that the Internet adds as much as $2 trillion to annual GDP, over $6,500 per person.

Another shortcoming of these models is that they fail to capture many of the most important innovations and developments occurring in sub-industries. Yet the U.S. has a history of innovating towards higher-wage jobs within industries. The experience of industries as diverse as semi-conductors and boatbuilding illustrate this point amply (see Boxes 2 and 3).

We see an American future where this process of innovation in next-generation technologies and

> **Box 3. Boat Builders along Maine's Eastern Coast**
>
> The Maine boat building industry is an example where innovation-led transformations occur on a smaller, more local scale. Maine boat builders have a 400-year heritage of skilled craftsmanship, but technological change was threatening to leave them behind. Instead, the boat builders have enthusiastically embraced cutting edge innovation in advanced composite technologies, replacing old jobs with better jobs in the same industry. Today, the Maine boat building industry produces a highly regarded product line that includes racing yachts, pleasure craft, workboats, and military vessels. As a result, wages in Maine's boat building industry have risen 19 in percent in real terms over the last decade while employment has risen 12 percent.

business ideas becomes pervasive, diffusing throughout the economy and generating better jobs and improved lives for all Americans. It is imperative that we turn this vision into a reality.

III –THE APPROPRIATE ROLE FOR GOVERNMENT

Framework for Government Involvement

While it is clear that a new foundation for innovation and growth is needed, the appropriate framework for government involvement is still debated. Some claim that the laissez-faire policies of the last decade approach the right strategy, and that the recent crisis was the result of too much rather than too little government support. This view calls for cutting government regulation and gutting public programs, hoping the market will take care of the rest.

However, the recent crisis illustrates that the free market itself does not promote the long-term benefit of society, and that certain fundamental investments and regulations are necessary to promote the social good. This is particularly true in the case of investments for research and development, where knowledge spillovers and other externalities ensure that the private sector will under-invest –especially in the most basic of research.

Another view is that the government must dominate certain sectors, protecting and insulating those areas thought to be drivers of future growth. This view calls for massive, sustained government investment supported by stringent oversight, dictating the type and direction of both public and private investments through mandates and bans.

But historical experience in this country and others clearly indicates that governments who try to pick winners and drive growth too often end up wasting resources and stifling rather than promoting innovation. This is in part due to the limited ability of the government to predict the future, but also because such exercises are distorted by lobbyists and rent seekers, which are more likely to favor backward looking industries than forward looking ones. In the United States such failures at picking winners and losers includes most prominently the Synthetic Fuel Corporation, a $20 billion Federal project in the 1980s that failed to provide the promised alternative to oil.

Therefore, we reject both sides of this unproductive and anachronistic debate. The true choice in innovation is not between government and no government, but about the right type of government involvement in support of innovation. A modern, practical approach recognizes both the need for fundamental support and the hazards of overzealous government intervention. The government should make sure individuals and businesses have the tools and support to take risks and innovate, but should not dictate what risks they take.

We propose to strike a balance by investing in the building blocks that only the government can provide, setting an open and competitive environment for businesses and individuals to experiment and grow, and by providing extra catalysts to jumpstart innovation in sectors of national importance. In this way, we will harness the inherent ingenuity of the American people and a dynamic private sector to generate innovations that help ensure the next expansion is more solid, broad-based, and beneficial than previous ones.

Examples of Successful Innovation Programs

We have been successful in the past, and we can be successful in the future. Take the example of DARPA, the historically innovative central research and development organization of the Defense Department. DARPA is tasked with maintaining U.S. technological superiority, and has a history of creating new industries in information technology and advanced manufacturing (see Box 4).

Box 4. DARPA's Successful Innovations

Thirty years ago, DARPA supported the creation of the internet's predecessor, ARPANET, despite discouragement from the private sector. Today, over 1.6 billion people use the Internet. DARPA's innovative research has created entirely new capabilities for the U.S. military such as stealth aircraft, GPS, the M-16 assault rifle, and night vision goggles. It has provided the foundation for new industries like optical networking, supercomputers, and design tools for computer chips. DARPA's commitment to high-risk, high-return research will help ensure America is prepared to meet the 21st century's national defense challenges while also catalyzing breakthroughs in technological innovations that will create new industries and improve people's lives.

Government support has also helped push America to the cutting edge in emerging fields such as nanotechnology, which involves engineering materials and devices on the atomic and molecular level (see Box 5).

The Administration is committed to strengthening and focusing investments in our world-class nanotechnology research and development pipeline; targeting support for nanotechnology transfer and facilitating commercial start-ups; and cross-disciplinary training and education of scientists and engineers in the new-generation workforce. This will enable us to capitalize on our investments and stay at the cutting edge of this rapidly growing technology.

This pattern of government support driving innovations that improve lives and catalyze industries is pervasive. Of the 88 U.S. entities that received "R&D 100 Awards" as the nation's best innovations in 2006, 77 had received government support. We must build on this record of successful support to build a new foundation for innovation and growth.

Box 5. The Growing Fields of Nanotechnology and Personalized Medicine

A nanometer is a billionth of a meter – or one hundred thousand times smaller than the diameter of a human hair. Nanotechnology promises to transform multiple industries: capturing and storing clean energy, developing next-generation computer chips, early detection of diseases, smart anti-cancer therapeutics that deliver drugs only to tumor cells, and enabling all-new approaches to a wide range of manufacturing activities, among many other examples. While the commercial impact of nanotechnology to date has been limited primarily to nanomaterials applied to a range of consumer goods from healthcare and food products to textiles, automotive composites and industrial coatings, nanotechnology innovation is beginning to accelerate. The ten-year history of U.S. leadership in fundamental nanotechnology research and development under the National Nanotechnology Initiative has laid the crucial groundwork for developing commercial applications and scaling up production, creating demand for many new nanotechnology and manufacturing jobs in the near-term.

Nanotechnology is being applied in the developing medical engineering and personalized medicine industries. The practice of tailoring medical treatment to an individual's unique genetic make-up makes not only treatment, but early detection and prevention, more effective. It also reduces medical costs in cases where expensive treatments are unnecessary or futile. Researchers are currently experimenting with nanotechnology to develop drugs capable of targeting a disease without triggering the body's natural immune response.

The federal government's support has been essential in the development of this technology and this industry. The NIH, a major supporter of medical research, saw its budget increase 163% from 1993 to 2003 before stagnating until this year. President Obama has reversed the recent trend with $10 billion in additional NIH funding in the Recovery Act and a pledge for more sustained increases going forward. This funding will help these emerging industries flourish.

IV –A STRATEGY FOR AMERICAN INNOVATION

For our communities and for our country to thrive in this new century, we need to harness the spirit of innovation and discovery that has always moved America forward. We must foster innovation that will lead to the technologies of the future – which will in turn lead to the industries and jobs of the future.

President Obama has already taken historic steps to lay the foundation for the innovation economy of the future. In the Recovery Act alone the President committed over $100 billion to support groundbreaking innovation with investments in energy, basic research, education and training, advanced vehicle technology, innovative programs, health IT and health research, high speed rail, smart grid, and information technology (see Figure 1). His commitment also includes broader support in the Recovery Act and in his FY2010 budget on initiatives from education to infrastructure. The President's commitment is not just limited to more government funding, but extends to important regulatory and executive order initiatives such as patent reform, coordinated fuel efficiency standards, net neutrality, permit policy for offshore wind farms, and naming the first ever Chief Technology Officer of the U.S. Government.

Figure 1. Innovation Funding in the Recovery Act

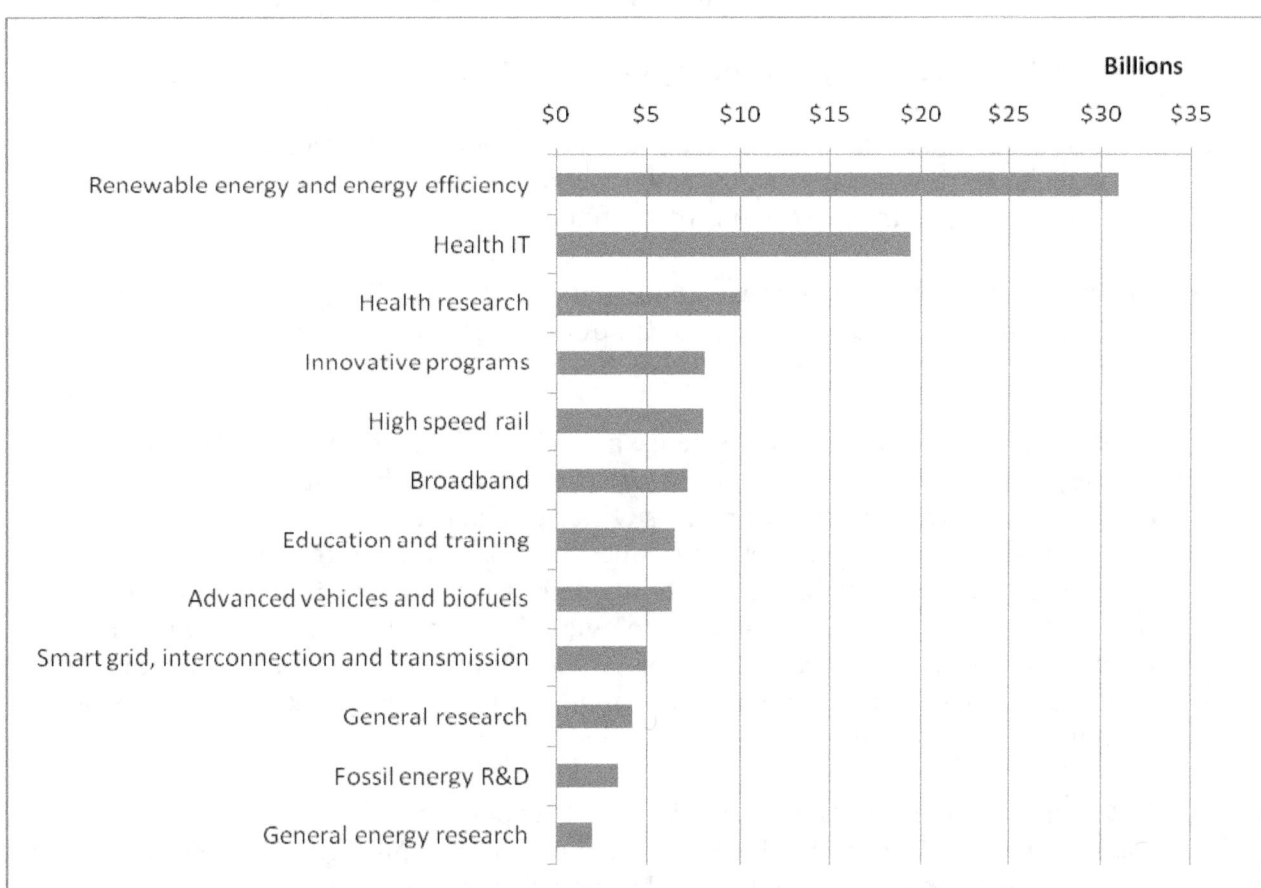

These investments and initiatives are part of The Obama Innovation Strategy, which focuses on critical areas where sensible, balanced government policies can lay the foundation for innovation that leads to quality jobs and shared prosperity. It has three parts:

1. **Invest in the Building Blocks of American Innovation.** We must first ensure that our economy is given all the necessary tools for successful innovation, from investments in research and development to the human, physical, and technological capital needed to perform that research and transfer those innovations.

2. **Promote Competitive Markets that Spur Productive Entrepreneurship.** It is imperative to create a national environment ripe for entrepreneurship and risk taking that allows U.S. companies to be internationally competitive in a global exchange of ideas and innovation. Through competitive markets, innovations diffuse and scale appropriately across industries and globally.

3. **Catalyze Breakthroughs for National Priorities.** There are certain sectors of exceptional national importance where the market is unlikely to produce the desirable outcomes on its own. These include developing alternative energy sources, reducing costs and improving lives with health IT, and manufacturing advanced vehicles. In these industries where markets may fail on their own, government can be part of the solution.

1. INVEST IN THE BUILDING BLOCKS OF AMERICAN INNOVATION

A. <u>Restore American Leadership in Fundamental Research</u>

President Obama recognizes the fundamental role of government in fostering groundbreaking scientific and technological breakthroughs, and has committed resources and energy to ensure America leads the world in the innovations of the future.

- **Enact the Largest R&D increase in our nation's history.** With $18.3 billion in research funding, the Recovery Act is part of the largest annual increase in research and development in America's history.

- **Double the R&D budget of key science agencies.** The President's Budget proposed to double the research budgets of three key science agencies: the National Science Foundation, the Department of Energy's Office of Science, and the National Institutes of Standards and Technology. These investments will expand the frontiers of human knowledge and create the foundation for the industries and jobs of the future, such as the convergence of bio, info, and nanotechnologies. The Obama Administration will increase the impact of this investment by providing more support for high-risk, high-return research, for multidisciplinary research, and for scientists and engineers at the beginning of their careers.

- **Invest three percent of GDP in R&D**. The President has proposed a goal that as a country, we invest more than three percent of our GDP in public and private research and development. This will exceed the level achieved at the height of the space race.

- **Make the R&E tax credit permanent.** The President's Budget includes the full $75 billion cost of making the research and experimentation tax credit permanent. This will provide businesses with the greater confidence they need to invest, innovate, and grow.

B. <u>Educate the Next Generation with 21st Century Knowledge and Skills While Creating a World-Class Workforce</u>

America's high levels of education were an important contributor to rising living standards in recent years. For America to continue to lead the world in science and technology innovation, it must have the most knowledgeable and skilled workers in the world.

- **Reform public schools to deliver a complete and competitive education.** The President is committed to an education system that will prepare every child for success in a new, global economy. The Obama Administration is supporting the improvement of teaching and learning to ensure that students master world-class knowledge and critical skills for the 21st century; enhance and reward success in the teaching profession; drive innovation in America's classrooms; and expand successful models to improve outcomes for middle- and high-school students. The President's Race to the Top in America's schools will deliver a historic investment and challenge the states to design and enforce higher and clearer standards, attract and keep outstanding teachers in the classroom, and use effective approaches to turn America's lowest-performing schools around.

- **Restore America to first in the world in college graduates**. Colleges, universities, and their students are bedrocks of American innovation. President Obama has called for restoring America to first in the world in the proportion of college graduates by 2020. Between the Recovery Act and the 2010 budget, the Administration is seeking nearly $200 billion over the next decade for scholarships and tax credits to help students complete college. The Obama Administration is investing in innovative strategies to support college persistence, simplify the student aid application and reform the student loan program to shift billions in wasteful spending toward greater help for students to reach and complete college. The Administration has been actively working with Congress to fund these priorities by eliminating waste in the student aid program.

- **Improve America's Science, Technology, Engineering and Math (STEM) education.** STEM education is particularly important to America's future scientific progress and economic growth. As part of his effort to promote innovation in K-12 education, the President has challenged governors, philanthropists, scientists, engineers, educators and the private sector to join with him to dramatically improve achievement in STEM subjects. The President's Race to the Top fund aims to reinvigorate the teaching of STEM in America's classrooms and support advanced learning in these subjects, especially for women, girls and other underrepresented groups. The President is also committed to using the $4 billion Race to the Top fund to encourage states to put STEM at the center of their reform efforts. Finally, the Recovery Act provided a down payment toward the goal of tripling the number of NSF Graduate Research Fellowships in science and engineering.

- **Develop new career pathways in community college programs**. Given the innovation and advances coming in future years, jobs requiring at least an associate's degree are projected to grow twice as fast as those requiring no college experience. President Obama has proposed the American Graduation Initiative to produce 5 million more community college graduates by 2020, a key part of his college completion goal. The initiative would invest in promising reforms to raise graduation rates, tie courses to business needs, improve remedial education and strengthen transitions with high schools and four-year colleges. It would also leverage $10 billion in facilities modernization and repairs amongst other projects.

- **Design world-class online courses for post-secondary students**. The President is proposing to invest up to $500 million over the next 10 years to create world-class online courses available at community colleges for students to gain knowledge, skills and

11

credentials. These courses will be freely available, and enable students to extend learning opportunities and successfully complete their course work. Colleges, universities, publishers, and other groups will be invited to compete to create state-of-the-art online courses that combine high-quality subject matter expertise with the latest advances in cognitive and computer sciences.

- **Improve the processing of high-tech visas.** In order to maintain our role as a global leader and convener of scientific conferences and other gatherings, the Obama Administration has worked to ensure foreign scientists and technological leaders can visit the United States to participate in important events while continuing to protect sensitive technologies.

C. Build a Leading Physical Infrastructure

The President has committed to a historic investment in our nation's roads, bridges, transit, and air networks to connect our people and our businesses.

- **Invest in our nation's roads, bridges, and mass transit.** The Recovery act provides $36 billion for infrastructure projects to improve our nation's highways and mass transit systems. The Obama Administration has also proposed "investing for performance" reforms that will improve transparency and accountability in the transportation financing system. Specific reform measures include building state and metropolitan project evaluation capabilities, improving project assessment tools, and creating stronger public reporting requirements. These reforms will promote accountability in the transportation financing system and increase the return to transportation investments, thereby boosting long-term economic growth.

- **Modernize the Electric Grid.** Our current electricity transmission grid must be expanded and modernized to reduce congestion, maintain reliability, and accommodate the output from new sources of renewable energy. New technologies are being developed that present significant opportunities for consumers and businesses to control their energy use and costs, reducing the strain on the electric grid and improving performance. The Recovery Act provides $4.5 billion for the development of technologies to enable greater energy efficiency, customer demand response, energy storage, and other components of the "Smart Grid." The Recovery Act increased the borrowing authority of the Bonneville Power Authority by $3.25 billion and provided new borrowing authority of $3.25 billion for the Western Area Power Authority, enabling both Authorities to invest in transmission lines that will increase the development of renewables in their regions.

- **Fulfill a new transportation vision with high-speed rail.** The President has proposed a long-term strategy to build an efficient, high-speed rail network of 100-600 mile intercity corridors, as one element of a modernized transportation system. The President made a down payment on this strategy with an $8 billion investment in the Recovery Act. This will be used to leverage other public and private funding to invest in infrastructure, equipment, and intermodal connections along three tracks.

First, the strategy will advance new express high-speed corridor services (operating at speeds above 150 mph in some areas) in select corridors of 200-600 miles. Second, the strategy will develop emerging and regional high-speed corridor services (operating at speeds between 90 and 150 mph) in corridors of 100 to 500 miles. And third, the strategy will upgrade the reliability and service on conventional intercity rail services (operating at speeds up to 79-90 mph).

The President has also budgeted for another $1 billion per year to continue to develop the high-speed rail network.

- **Develop the next generation of air traffic control.** The FY2010 Budget provides $865 million for the Next Generation Air Transportation System in the Federal Aviation Administration. The Administration supports moving from a ground-based radar surveillance system to a more accurate satellite-based surveillance system, the development of more efficient routes through the airspace, and improvements in aviation weather information.

D. Develop an Advanced Information Technology Ecosystem

For America to lead the world in the technologies of the future, President Obama believes that all Americans must have affordable 21st century access to the Internet.

- **Expand access to broadband.** The Recovery Act provides $7.2 billion for broadband expansion and the 2010 budget includes $1.3 billion in USDA loans and grants to increase broadband capacity and telecommunication service. This support is a kickstart towards ensuring that all Americans have affordable 21st century access to the Internet. Widespread high-speed Internet access is essential for economic growth, job creation, and global competitiveness, and will foster the next generation of innovators while enabling reductions in energy consumption through telework, making online distance education tools accessible to all, enhancing remote medical monitoring capabilities, facilitating civic engagement, and supporting enhanced communications networks for first responders.

  Increased broadband access is a key input for rural economic development. It will enable rural businesses to improve their efficiency and expand their market reach; enable rural populations to compete remotely for a wide range of service jobs; and allow rural communities to retain their populations while attracting new businesses. The farm sector, a pioneer in rural Internet use, is increasingly comprised of farm businesses that purchase inputs and make sales online. Only 46 percent of adults in rural households have broadband access, compared to 67 percent for non-rural adults. America should lead the world in broadband adoption and Internet access, and we should not leave rural populations behind.

- **Assure net neutrality to preserve the freedom and openness of Internet access.** The Internet is the ultimate level playing field, making possible the widest and most lucrative variety of entrepreneurial activity and innovation that the world has ever seen. FCC Chairman Julius Genachowski announced on September 21st that providers of Internet access should not discriminate against lawful applications or content. We want to make sure it remains possible for anyone to start a business in a garage that creates new jobs, new ideas, and new opportunities for Americans. Our nation's economy is increasingly dependent on the Internet; the Internet is an essential infrastructure, like roads and electricity; and the global leadership that America provides today stems directly from historic policies that have ensured that telecommunications networks are open to all lawful uses by all users. That's the way the Internet has always worked, and we want it to stay that way – not because we treasure our past, but because we care about our economic future.

- **Support research for next-generation information and communications technology.** The Administration is committed to supporting research that will foster the next wave of innovation in information and communications technologies, such as "cognitive radio" that allows for the efficient sharing of spectrum, quantum computing, efficient programming of parallel computers, cyber-physical systems, secure computers and networks, data-intensive supercomputers, and nanoelectronics that enables the continuation of Moore's Law for decades to come. The President's Budget supports this research through grants for the National Science Foundation, DARPA, and other public and private institutions.

- **Appoint a Chief Technology Officer of the U.S. Government**. In April, President Obama named the first ever Chief Technology Officer of the U.S. government. The CTO position was created to oversee the application of technology to create jobs and spur economic growth. The Administration is committed to recruiting high-level champions for innovation across the government.

- **Secure cyberspace**. The President has identified cybersecurity as a national priority to ensure that cyberspace – the globally-interconnected digital communications infrastructure - is sufficiently resilient and trustworthy to support U.S. goals of economic growth, civil liberties, privacy protections, national security, and the continued advancement of democratic institutions. Leadership in this effort has been anchored in the White House through the positions of the U.S. Chief Technology Officer, the U.S. Chief Information Officer, and the President's coming Cybersecurity Coordinator. This leadership team is partnering across the public and private sectors to build capacity for a digital nation through education, training and awareness; enhance security through information sharing, effective incident response planning, and privacy-enhancing identity management strategies; and encourage innovation through game-changing research and development strategies.

2. PROMOTE COMPETITIVE MARKETS THAT SPUR PRODUCTIVE ENTREPRENEURSHIP

A. Promote American Exports

Exports will play an increasingly critical role in the future of the American economy, and the President's plans will ensure fair and open markets for American producers.

- **Open markets abroad.** The Obama Administration is working with our trading partners to negotiate mutually beneficial trade agreements and to maintain the worldwide flow of goods, services, and capital. Only by keeping markets open can American producers sell to world markets and derive the benefits of participating in an open exchange of ideas and innovations.

- **Promote American Exports.** President Obama is committed to robust support for American exporters. The United States Trade Representative (USTR) and the Department of Commerce are proactively coordinating our support through programs such as the International Trade Administration and the Trade Promotion Coordinating Committee.

- **Enforce our trade agreements to ensure access for American products abroad.** Over the last eight years the enforcement of trade agreements slowed dramatically, with the United States bringing only an average of three WTO cases per year – as opposed to the approximately 11 annually from 1995 to 2001. In this era, the United States lost its focus on ensuring that other countries lived up to their promises to open their markets, not violate America's intellectual property, and not use dumping or subsidies to penetrate America's markets. Under President Obama, USTR and the Department of Commerce are committed to a new emphasis on enforcing our existing agreements.

- **Protect intellectual property rights.** Intellectual property is to the digital age what physical goods were to the industrial age. We must ensure that intellectual property is protected in foreign markets and promote greater cooperation on international standards that allow our technologies to compete everywhere. The Administration is committed to ensuring that the United States Patent and Trademark Office has the resources, authority, and flexibility to administer the patent system effectively and issue high-quality patents on innovative intellectual property, while rejecting claims that do not merit patent protection.

- **Reform U.S. export controls.** The President has directed that the National Economic Council and the National Security Council review the overall U.S. export control system, tasking them to consider reforms that enhance America's national security, foreign policy, and economic security interests. While the U.S. has one of the most robust export control systems in the world, it remains rooted in the Cold War era of over 50 years ago. It must be updated to address the threats we face today and the changing economic and technological landscape.

B. <u>Support Open Capital Markets that Allocate Resources to the Most Promising Ideas</u>

Open capital markets are one of the greatest strengths of the American economy, and the President is committed to making sure these markets work.

- **Promote open capital markets.** In our economic system, freely moving capital searchers for the most promising innovations to nurture and propel. Providing American leadership in well regulated, open markets will support global technology development, and the President is committed to this system.

- **Ensure working financial markets.** While free and open markets provide significant benefits, they must work for consumers and investors. The recent financial crisis highlighted the danger of managing a 21st century economy with a 20th century regulatory framework. We are committed to building a system where individuals and businesses can innovate and take chances without fearing that the system will pose untenable risks. Our plan:

  - Requires that all financial firms that pose a significant risk to the financial system at large are subjected to consolidated supervision and regulation.
  - Increases supervision of financial markets to help ensure that our markets are strong enough to withstand system-wide stress and the potential failure of one or more large financial institutions.
  - Rebuilds trust in our markets by creating a Consumer Financial Protection Agency to focus exclusively on protecting consumers in credit, savings, and payment markets.
  - Provides the government with the tools to cope with crises by ensuring the orderly unwinding of failing firms and avoiding the untenable choice between bailouts or damaging collapse.
  - Raises international regulatory standards and improves international coordination.

C. Encourage High-Growth and Innovation-Based Entrepreneurship

Entrepreneurship has played, and will continue to play, an essential role in generating innovation and stimulating U.S. economic growth. Firms with fewer than 20 employees accounted for approximately 18 percent of private sector jobs in 2006, but nearly 25 percent of net employment growth from 1992 to 2005. Small businesses employ 30% of high tech workers such as scientists, engineers, and information technology workers. The Obama Administration is committed to helping entrepreneurs build new and vibrant businesses that lead to new jobs and economic growth.

- **Increase access to capital for new businesses.** Providing access to credit for entrepreneurs and small business owners is a foundational element of economic recovery and growth. The Recovery Act reduced fees and increased guarantee levels on small business loans, while the U.S. Small Business Administration (SBA) has increased small business lending by more than 61% from the depths of the recession while broadening the base of commercial SBA lenders. Growth capital is essential. The Small Business Investment Company (SBIC) Debentures program provides debt and mezzanine financing at a time when the equity markets have pulled back from providing capital to these companies. The President has also proposed eliminating the capital gains tax on small businesses.

- **Provide training and mentoring to entrepreneurs.** Entrepreneurs with access to a network of trainers, mentors, and counselors can improve their chances for success in building high-growth businesses. The SBA has 68 district offices and over a thousand nonprofit "resource partners" that offer 14,000 counselors who serve about 1.5 million entrepreneurs and small business owners each year. The Administration is partnering with community colleges, universities, and the philanthropic sector to deliver more training and mentoring resources to aspiring entrepreneurs to promote the creation of new businesses, particularly among women and minorities.

- **Create competitive communities by promoting regional innovation clusters.** In various regions of the U.S., entrepreneurs are collaborating with local researchers, educators and industry leaders to foster specialized knowledge, technical expertise, and cutting-edge products. This will help American businesses retain and achieve new levels of competitiveness. The President's Budget provides $50 million in regional planning and matching grants within the Economic Development Administration (EDA) to support the creation of regional innovation clusters that leverage regions' existing competitive strengths to boost job creation and economic growth. The Budget also launches a $50 million initiative in EDA that will create a national network of business incubators to encourage entrepreneurial activity in economically distressed areas.

- **Stimulate entrepreneurship through increased access to government data.** The Administration launched Data.gov, a one-stop shop for free access to data generated across all Federal agencies. By empowering the American people to find, use, and repackage data, Data.gov will give rise to new businesses (like the GPS and genomics industries that grew from increased access to public information) and empower entrepreneurs to evaluate opportunities.

- **Protect small businesses from unfair business practices.** In many industries, small companies are critical innovators, bringing enormous benefits to consumers while putting competitive pressure on incumbent firms. The Obama Administration is committed to enforcing the antitrust laws to insure that innovative entrepreneurs are not excluded from the market by anti-competitive conduct. The Department of Justice actively investigates allegations of exclusionary conduct as part of its law enforcement mission to keep markets open and competitive.

D. Improve Public Sector Innovation and Support Community Innovation

Innovation must occur within all levels of society, including the government and civil society. The Obama Administration is committed to increasing the ability of government to promote and harness innovation. The Administration is encouraging departments and agencies to experiment with new technologies that have the potential to increase efficiency and reduce expenditures, such as cloud computing. The Federal government should take advantage of the expertise and insight of people both inside and outside the Federal government, use high-risk, high-reward policy tools such as prizes and challenges to solve tough problems, support the broad adoption of community solutions that work, and form high-impact collaborations with researchers, the private sector, and civil society.

- **Make the government more transparent, participatory, and collaborative.** On his first day in office, the President signed the Memorandum on Transparency and Open Government, thereby placing government accountability and civic engagement at the forefront of the Administration's governing philosophy. The President's Memorandum urged agencies to promote three principles for bringing innovation to government: transparency, participation, and collaboration. Transparency promotes accountability by providing citizens with information about what their Government is doing. Public participation in decision-making strengthens democracy and ensures that Government makes policies with the benefit of information that is widely dispersed in society. Collaboration improves the effectiveness of Government by encouraging cooperation and knowledge-sharing within the Federal Government, across levels of Government and between the Government and private institutions.

- **Promote Open Government**. The Administration created the White House Open Government Initiative to coordinate Open Government policy, projects, and design technology platforms that foster openness across the Executive branch. The Initiative has achieved many important milestones, including:

  - Publishing government data online to make it easy for anyone to remix and reuse, thus involving the American people in the development of public policy,
  - Challenging thousands of Federal employees to propose ideas for slashing the time required to process veterans' disability benefits,
  - Releasing information on Executive branch personnel and salaries, and
  - Launching the IT dashboard, a one-stop clearinghouse of information that allows anyone with a web browser to track government spending on technology and hold the government accountable.

- **Use innovation to improve government programs.** President Obama is committed to using novel techniques and research support to improve the efficiency and effectiveness of government programs. For example, the Recovery Act includes a $7 billion fund to incentivize innovative reforms in states' Unemployment Insurance programs. States that use the most recent wage data and commit to cover more groups of job seekers get rewarded with higher payments. Already 32 states have qualified, and of these 24 of them changed their laws to do so. Another example is support for patient-centered health research in the Recovery Act. This research will lead to higher quality and more effective ways to deliver healthcare. The results will stimulate action across the health system to incorporate these findings into programs.

- **Commit White House Resources to scaling and promoting community innovations**. The President created the White House Office of Social Innovation and Civic Participation to grow the marketplace for community innovations and provide the technology and tools for greater civic participation to help tackle our nation's toughest problems. The office will build upon efforts across the agencies, such as the Department of Education's $650 million Invest in Innovation (i3) Fund, to create new models of Federal grant-making that focus on encouraging, testing and scaling the most promising ideas and programs. The office uses its convening power to coordinate and partner with citizens, philanthropists, and the private sector to create a supportive environment for on-going innovations in communities. Part of the effort will include using innovative tools such as prizes and challenges. The President's Budget includes $50 million in seed capital for the nation's first Social Innovation Fund, which will identify the most promising, results-oriented non-profit programs and provide the capital needed to replicate their success in communities around the country.

3. CATALYZE BREAKTHROUGHS FOR NATIONAL PRIORITIES

A. <u>Unleash a Clean Energy Revolution</u>

President Obama is committed to U.S. leadership in the new clean energy economy of the future. The Administration's investments will put American innovators ahead of the curve, creating new jobs in cutting edge industries while tackling the threat posed by climate change.

- **Double the nation's supply of renewable energy in the next three years.** The President has set a goal to double the generation of renewable energy in the next three years, unleashing a wave of innovation in the clean energy industries of the future. To accomplish this vision, the Recovery Act included billions of dollars to support loan guarantees and the extension of the Production Tax Credit for electricity production from renewable energy sources, leveraging tens of billions of dollars in private investment. The Recovery Act and the President's 2010 Budget also include significant increases for renewable energy technology R&D. In addition, the President pursued regulatory reform to ease the transition to a clean energy economy. In April the Department of the Interior released final regulations that will govern the development of renewable energy in offshore waters. These rules will enable our Nation to tap into the ocean's vast sustainable resources to generate clean, green energy in an environmentally sound and safe manner.

- **Promote energy efficient industries.** The Recovery Act and national energy policy will generate a proliferation of new technologies, processes, and jobs relating to improving energy efficiency. The Recovery Act alone provided $5 billion in funding for weatherization assistance to low-income residents, $4.5 billion for greening Federal buildings, and $6.3 billion for state and local government renewable energy and energy efficiency and conservation efforts.

- **Invest in Clean energy innovation**. The President has proposed a 10 year, $150 billion investment in the research, development and demonstration of clean energy technologies, such as solar, wind, green buildings, efficient lighting, next-generation biofuels, proliferation-resistant nuclear reactors, energy storage, and carbon capture and storage.

- **Enact a cap-and-trade program to curb oil dependence and greenhouse gas emissions while spurring renewable energy technologies.** President Obama supports a comprehensive cap-and-trade program that will provide a clear signal that the current energy mix is unacceptable and that low-carbon energy sources are the way of the future. The program will provide the certainty necessary for businesses to make transformative investments in renewable alternatives and energy efficiency.

- **RE-ENERGYSE the American workforce.** The President has proposed RE-ENERGYSE, a joint educational campaign from the Department of Energy and the National Science Foundation to inspire tens of thousands of young Americans to pursue careers in clean energy. RE-ENERGYSE will support fellowships, interdisciplinary graduate programs, and partnerships between academic institutions and innovative companies to prepare a generation of Americans to meet the energy challenge.

B. Support Advanced Vehicle Technologies

For the sake of our national security, economy, and environment, it is crucial to diversify away from oil as the sole source of transportation fuel. Today, oil accounts for 96 percent of the fuel that powers our country's vehicle fleet. The lack of widespread, affordable alternatives to oil makes us vulnerable to market disruptions and dependent on oil producers. Oil is also responsible for one third of our carbon dioxide emissions and is a significant source of local air pollution, threatening our climate security and the health of our local communities.

The President's strategy is to put the U.S. at the cutting edge of the advanced vehicle technology industry, which will not only reduce our dependence on oil, but will also create jobs, strengthen our manufacturing base, improve the quality of the air we breathe, and offer consumers greater safety, performance, and choice.

- **Make the largest investment in technology for electric vehicles and transportation electrification in U.S. history.** In early August the Administration announced $2 billion in grants which will catalyze private sector investment to build a globally competitive domestic battery and electric drive component industry. With this support, American factories will produce the lightest, cheapest, longest-lasting, and most powerful vehicle batteries in the world. American batteries and components will power affordable electric cars that can travel over hundred miles on a single charge and offer customers superb performance. These vehicles will be even more attractive thanks to the tax credit of up to $7,500 offered for electric and plug-in electric vehicles in the Recovery Act.

  The Administration is also making a $400 million holistic investment in transportation electrification as a system. Beyond batteries, vehicles, and components, this includes demonstrating pilot systems that put the pieces together – testing the infrastructure to plug the cars, training the workers to build and service them, and educating the consumers who will buy them. The lessons from these projects will help the private sector more quickly develop profitable electric vehicles that meet the needs of drivers.

- **Deploy up to $25 billion in loans to support American manufacturing of advanced vehicle technologies.** Through the $25 billion Advanced Technology Vehicles Manufacturing Loan Program, the Administration is supporting competition within the marketplace to produce the most cost-effective solutions to reduce oil dependence. The Administration awarded the first $8 billion in conditional loan commitments in June. These included $5.9 billion for Ford Motor Company to transform factories across Illinois, Kentucky, Michigan, Missouri, and Ohio to produce 13 more fuel efficient models; $1.6 billion to Nissan North America, Inc. to retool their Smyrna, Tennessee factory to build advanced electric automobiles and to build an advanced battery manufacturing facility; and $465 million to Tesla Motors to manufacture electric drive trains and electric vehicles in California. Up to an additional $17 billion in loans will be made under this program over the next several years.

- **Support the next generation of American biofuels.** The Administration is investing in next generation biofuels that displace oil consumption and reduce greenhouse gas emissions. Through $800 million in Recovery Act grants as well as up to $500 million to support loan guarantees, the Administration is accelerating the development of clean technologies like cellulosic and algae-based biofuels –harnessing recent advances in synthetic biology.

- **Improve vehicle fuel efficiency to reduce oil dependence and spark innovation.** In May, President Obama announced a groundbreaking national autos program that put us on a path to adopting uniform Federal standards to regulate both fuel economy and greenhouse gas emissions. The result will be a projected reduction in oil consumption of approximately 1.8 billion barrels over the life of the program and a projected total reduction in greenhouse gas emissions of approximately 950 million metric tons. This landmark policy will spark innovation in more fuel-efficient vehicles, reduce pollution, and promote energy security.

C. Drive Innovations in Health Care Technology

The inefficiencies in our health care system raise costs and reduce the quality of care. New advances in health information technology will increase efficiency while broad reform will free businesses and individuals to innovate and grow.

- **Expand the use of health IT.** Expanded use of advanced health information technology (e.g. electronic medical records, mobile health applications, sensors for monitoring chronic diseases) will help prevent medical errors, improve health care quality, begin to modernize the American health care system and reduce costs. The Recovery Act provides over $19 billion in investments to modernize health information technology.

- **Renew our commitment to medical research.** The Recovery act included a $10 billion expansion in health research. This will fund projects such as an initiative to identify all of the genetic changes involved in 20 types of cancer, clinical trials of medicines that could help stop the HIV/AIDS pandemic, the largest infusion of funding to discover the causes and treatment for autism, and using DNA sequencing to discover how to prevent and treat heart, lung, and blood diseases

- **Slow the growth of health care costs.** The President is committed to comprehensive reform for a health care system that makes it possible to improve the quality of care while slowing the growth rate of costs. Doing this will free up resources that can be used to invest in American businesses and improve the living standards for all Americans.

D. Harness Science and Technology to Address the "Grand Challenges" of the 21st Century

The President's renewed commitment to science, technology and innovation will allow the nation to set and meet ambitious goals that will improve our quality of life and establish the foundation for the industries and jobs of the future. Examples include:

- Complete DNA sequencing of every case of cancer; smart anti-cancer therapeutics that kill cancer cells and leave their normal neighbors untouched; early detection of dozens of diseases from a saliva sample; nanotechnology that delivers drugs precisely to the desired tissue; personalized medicine that enables the prescription of the right dose of the right drug for the right person; a universal vaccine for influenza that will protect against all future strains; and regenerative medicine that can end the agonizing wait for an organ transplant.

- Solar cells as cheap as paint, and green buildings that produce all of the energy they consume.

- A light-weight vest for soldiers and police officers that can stop an armor-piercing bullet.

- Educational software that is as compelling as the best video game and as effective as a personal tutor; online courses that improve the more students use them; and a rich, interactive digital library at the fingertips of every child.

- Intelligent prosthetics that will allow a veteran who has lost both of his arms to play the piano again.

- Biological systems that can turn sunlight into carbon-neutral fuel, reduce the costs of producing anti-malarial drugs by a factor of 10, and quickly and inexpensively dispose of radioactive wastes and toxic chemicals.

- An "exascale" supercomputer capable of a million trillion calculations per second – dramatically increasing our ability to understand the world around us through simulation and slashing the time needed to design complex products such as therapeutics, advanced materials, and highly-efficient autos and aircraft.

- Automatic, highly accurate and real-time translation between the major languages of the world – greatly lowering the barriers to international commerce and collaboration.